Healthy Eating on A Budget

How to Create a Nutritious Diet Plan Without Breaking the Bank

By Louis K. Ray

Table of Contents

Introduction

Eating healthily on a budget is an essential aspect of sustaining a healthy lifestyle. It is feasible to eat nutritiously and keep within your budget. Eating healthily may be a problem for many, particularly those on a limited budget. Eating healthy does not have to be costly or time demanding. With a little bit of forethought, healthy eating on a budget is feasible.

Our objective is to give you the tools and information to make healthy eating on a budget a reality. In this tutorial, we will cover how to make healthy eating on a budget a reality. We will explore the benefits of healthy eating and how to purchase smartly. We will also share suggestions on meal planning, cooking, and buying methods.

Eating well is crucial for many reasons. Eating well may help you maintain a healthy weight, minimize your risk of chronic illnesses, and improve your overall health. Eating healthily may also be advantageous to your budget. Eating nutritious meals that are abundant in nutrients will help you save money in the long term as compared to purchasing processed and unhealthy snacks.

Shopping wisely is crucial when attempting to eat healthily on a budget. Knowing what to look for and where to purchase may make all the difference. We will address the significance of reading labels, purchasing in bulk, and shopping at farmers' markets.

Meal planning is another way to make healthy eating on a budget a reality. Meal planning allows you to have a plan for the week and helps you to avoid unhealthy impulse purchases. We will cover how to design a meal plan that meets your budget and includes healthy, nutritional meals.

This guide will give you the knowledge you need to make healthy food choices while keeping within your budget. It will explain how to buy wisely, give recommendations on how to save money while grocery shopping, and provide meal choices that are both nutritional and cost-effective. With enough forethought and imagination, you can cook wonderful dinners without breaking the wallet.

Chapter 1

Benefits of Eating Healthy on a Budget

Eating healthily on a budget has numerous good implications for both physical and emotional health. Eating a balanced, healthy diet is vital for general health and well-being. Eating healthy on a budget can help you stay within your budget while still eating nutritious meals.

1. Lower Risk of Chronic Diseases: Eating a healthy, balanced diet can help reduce the risk of developing chronic diseases such as heart disease, stroke, diabetes, and obesity.

Eating healthy on a budget allows you to purchase nutrient-rich foods such as lean proteins, whole grains, fruits, vegetables, and legumes, which are all important for preventing and managing chronic diseases.

2. Improved Physical Performance: Eating healthy on a budget can help improve physical performance. Nutrient-rich foods provide the body with essential vitamins, minerals, and macronutrients that are important for improving physical performance and energy levels. Eating healthily on a budget may help you satisfy your body's nutritional demands without breaking your wallet.

3. Improved Mental Health: Eating well on a budget may enhance mental health by

lowering stress levels, enhancing mood, and increasing cognitive function. When you can acquire nutrient-rich meals, your body can absorb the required vitamins and minerals to help keep your mind and body sharp. Eating healthily on a budget might help you acquire the nutrients you need to be mentally healthy.

4. Reduced Risk of Weight Gain: Consuming healthily on a budget may help lower the risk of weight gain by eating nutrient-rich foods that are low in calories and high in vital elements. Eating healthily on a budget enables you to select nutrient-rich foods that are low in calories, but still include necessary vitamins and minerals.

Overall, eating healthily on a budget may have many favorable consequences on physical and mental health. Eating a balanced, healthy diet is vital for general health and well-being. Eating healthily on a budget might help you keep within your budget while still eating nutritional meals.

Chapter 2

Set a Realistic Budget

Setting a reasonable budget is a vital step to attaining financial success.

A realistic budget can help you manage your money more effectively, predict future demands, and prepare for long-term objectives. It is crucial to building a budget that is based on your existing income, spending, and lifestyle.

A budget should be routinely checked and updated to reflect changes in your financial status. By making a realistic budget, you can guarantee that you are in charge of your money and that you are taking the actions required to attain financial stability. It might be tough to stay on a budget, but with a few ideas, it can become an easy and pleasurable activity.

1. Know your income: Start by jotting down all of your sources of money and how much you earn each month. This will give you a decent notion of how much money you have to work with and how you should distribute it.

2. Assess your spending: Make a list of all of your expenses, including bills, food, entertainment, and any other required goods. This can help you find the areas where you may save money or make better decisions.

3. Create a budget limit: Once you have determined your income and spending, set a budget limit for each area. This will help you remain within your means and keep your spending in control.

4. Track your spending: Write down all of your purchases in a journal or spreadsheet. This can help you remain on top of your budget and discover areas where you are overpaying.

5. Establish a plan: Once you have recorded your expenditure, make a strategy for the future. Set objectives for yourself and change your spending limit appropriately.

6. Be flexible: Life occurs, and your budget may need to be altered from time to time. If you have an unexpected expenditure, attempt to minimize spending in other areas to remain inside your budget.

7 Reward yourself: Don't forget to reward yourself when you stay within your budget. A modest gift or reward might help you remain motivated and keep you on track.

Setting a realistic budget may be tough, but with a few basic steps, it can become an easy and pleasurable exercise. Taking the effort to monitor your expenditures and establish a strategy for the future can help you reach your financial objectives.

Chapter 3
Making Healthy Eating Affordable

Eating well is one of the most essential components of a healthy lifestyle, yet it can sometimes be costly and hard. Fortunately, there are methods to make healthy eating economical and simple. Here are some suggestions and techniques to help you make healthy eating economical.

Write a comprehensive ñote on making healthy eating economical via bulk shopping, producing your food, choosing in-season produce, making good use of leftovers, purchasing whole grain, storing up on canned and frozen food

Healthy eating may be a costly affair. But it doesn't have to be. Making healthy eating affordable is possible if you make use of the following strategies.

Buying food in bulk is a terrific method to save money on healthful goods such as grains, nuts, and dried fruit. You may discover bargains on bulk goods at most grocery shops and health food stores. You may also check online for bulk businesses that offer amazing bargains on healthy foods.

Growing Your Food: Growing your vegetables is a fantastic way to save money and eat healthier. You may acquire seeds and produce plants in your yard or even build up a container garden if you don't have a lot of room.

Choose In-Season Produce: Produce is often the most costly item on your shopping list. To save money, always select in-season products. In-season produce is often less costly than out-of-season food and frequently tastes better as well.

Make Good Use of Leftovers: Don't allow your leftovers to go to waste. Use them to prepare new dishes or freeze them for later. This will save you money and guarantee that you're eating nutritious meals.

Buy Whole Grain: Whole grains are healthier than processed grains. They are also frequently cheaper than processed grains. Look for whole-grain items such as brown rice, oats, and quinoa that are budget-friendly and healthy.

Stock Up on Canned and Frozen Food: Canned and frozen food can be a great way to save money and still eat healthily. Canned veggies, beans, and fruits are generally cheaper than fresh food and they last a long time. Frozen veggies and fruits are also an excellent alternative since they are frequently cheaper than fresh and just as healthy.

By employing these techniques, you can make healthy eating economical. Eating healthy doesn't have to be costly — with a little bit of planning and preparation, you can eat healthily on a budget.

Chapter 4

Recipes for Healthy Eating on a Budget

Breakfast Recipes for Healthy Eating on a Budget

Breakfast is the most important meal of the day and it is necessary to start your day off with a good and nutritious meal. Eating healthily on a budget might be tough, but it doesn't have to be. Here are some breakfast dishes that are both nutritious and inexpensive.

Egg Muffins: These egg muffins may be made in advance and then kept in the fridge or freezer. All you need are eggs, veggies, and any extra toppings you'd want. They are a wonderful grab-and-go breakfast alternative.

Banana Nut Protein Smoothie: This smoothie is filled with protein and other nutritional ingredients. All you need is banana, nut butter, protein powder, unsweetened almond milk, and ice.

Omelet with Vegetables: Start your day off properly with a protein-rich omelet loaded with veggies. Start with mixing eggs and milk, then pour into a heated pan with a little butter or oil. Add in your favorite choice of chopped vegetables, such as onions, peppers, tomatoes, spinach, mushrooms, and more. Cook until the eggs are set, then put them onto a dish and enjoy!

Yogurt Parfait: Start your day with a nutritious and tasty yogurt parfait. Layer Greek yogurt with fresh or frozen fruit, granola, and a sprinkle of honey. This quick meal is simple to cook and filled with protein and fiber.

Oats with Fruit: Oats are an excellent source of fiber and may be dressed up in several ways. Cook up a batch of oats with a mix of water and milk. Top with fresh or frozen fruit, nuts, seeds, and a drizzle of honey.

Lunch Recipes for Healthy Eating on a Budget

Making a nutritious lunch doesn't have to be costly or time-consuming. Here are some quick and economical lunch dishes that you can whip up in no time.

Tuna Salad Wraps: These wraps are a terrific way to use up any leftover tuna you have. Simply add some mayo, sliced onion, celery, and whatever other veggies you have on hand. Roll it up in a wrap and you're ready to go.

Quinoa Bowls: Quinoa bowls are a terrific way to pack in some protein and veggies. Simply prepare the quinoa according to package directions and then put in your favorite toppings such as roasted veggies, feta cheese, and a dressing of your choosing.

Chicken and Avocado Salad: This salad is a terrific way to use up any leftover chicken you have. Simply add some chopped chicken, diced avocado, diced onion, and a dressing of your choosing.

Veggie Wrap: A veggie wrap is a simple way to add extra veggies to your diet. Start with spreading a whole-wheat wrap with hummus, then top with your favorite choice of chopped vegetables. Roll it up and enjoy!

Leftovers: Don't forget to make the most of the leftovers! Reheat yesterday night's meal and enjoy it for lunch the following day.

Dinner Recipes for Healthy Eating on a Budget

Eating healthy doesn't have to be costly. Here are some supper dishes that are both healthy and inexpensive.

Baked Salmon: Salmon is a fantastic source of protein and healthy fats. To create this recipe, just season the salmon with your chosen spices and bake in the oven for 20 minutes. Serve with a side of roasted veggies for a full supper.

Stir-Fry: Stir-fries are a terrific way to use up any vegetables you have on hand. Start by sautéing in a heated pan with a little oil and garlic. Add in your favorite choice of chopped vegetables, such as onions, peppers, broccoli, mushrooms, and more. Once the vegetables are soft, put in cooked chicken, meat, or shrimp. Serve over brown rice or quinoa for a full dinner.

Baked Fish: Fish is a great source of lean protein and is easy to prepare. Start by preheating the oven to 375°F. Place your desired fish fillet on a baking sheet and season with salt and pepper. Top with your favorite herbs and a drizzle of olive oil and bake for 10-15 minutes, or until the fish is cooked through.

Pasta and Veggies: Pasta is a great way to get more veggies into your diet. Start by cooking your favorite pasta according to package instructions. In a separate pan, sauté an assortment of veggies in a little oil and garlic. Once the veggies are tender, add in cooked pasta and toss to combine. Add a sprinkle of Parmesan cheese and enjoy!

Turkey Burgers: For a lean alternative to beef burgers, make turkey burgers. Mix ground turkey, diced onions, garlic, and your favorite herbs and spices. Form into patties and grill or bake.

Snacks

Fruit and Nut Butter: Fruit and nut butter make a great snack. Start by slicing your favorite fruit, such as apples, bananas, or pears. Top with a spoonful of nut butter and enjoy!

Trail Mix: Make your trail mix using a variety of dried fruit, nuts, and seeds. This snack is quick to prepare and ideal for the on-the-go.

Popcorn: Popcorn is a nutritious and enjoyable snack. Make your own with a little oil and salt, or purchase pre-made.

Fruit Smoothie: Make a healthy and full smoothie using your favorite fruits, yogurt, and milk. This is a terrific method to obtain your daily dosage of vitamins and minerals.

Dessert

Fruit with Dark Chocolate: Satisfy your sweet desire with a nutritious treat. Slice your favorite fruit and top it with a couple of pieces of dark chocolate. The mix of fruit and dark chocolate is a fantastic approach to satiate your desires.

Yogurt Popsicles: Yogurt popsicles are a terrific way to cool down on a hot day. Start by blending plain yogurt with your favorite fruits and purée in a blender. Pour the mixture into popsicle molds and freeze until hardened. Enjoy!

Banana "Ice Cream": This healthful dish is a terrific way to fulfill your sweet appetite. Start by slicing a few ripe bananas and freezing until firm. Place the frozen banana slices in a food processor and pulse until smooth. Add in a little milk or cream for a creamy texture, then enjoy!

Baked Apples: Core one apple and fill it with a teaspoon of brown sugar, cinnamon, and raisins. Bake for 15 minutes @ 350F and enjoy.

Chapter 5

Conclusion

In conclusion, nutritious eating on a budget needs careful planning and savvy buying. It is possible to create a nutritious diet plan without breaking the bank. With a little bit of study, you may locate nutritious, economical meals that can fit into your budget. You may also build meal plans that incorporate economical, nutrient-rich items that can help you achieve your dietary demands.

Additionally, taking advantage of specials, coupons, and store brands might help you save money on groceries. Finally, being conscious of portion sizes and preferring nutrient-rich foods over unhealthy alternatives will help you keep within your budget while still eating healthily. Eating healthily on a budget is doable, and with careful planning and savvy buying, you can build a balanced diet plan without breaking the bank